Easy
KEYBOARD

Songs for Beginners

40 easy and fun tunes

Contents

Introduction

This collection of easy tunes for keyboard is designed for beginners as well as those who have more playing experience. The initial tunes use only 3 - 5 different notes but by the end of the book the tunes range to over an octave with some sharps and flats also being used.

Chords are suggested to go with each song although the tunes will all sound very good even without harmonies. (Elementary players will probably prefer to play just the tune). A chord chart is included at the back of this book.

For those who are still learning to read the music and remember which note is which the following reference chart shows how to find all of the notes used in this book:

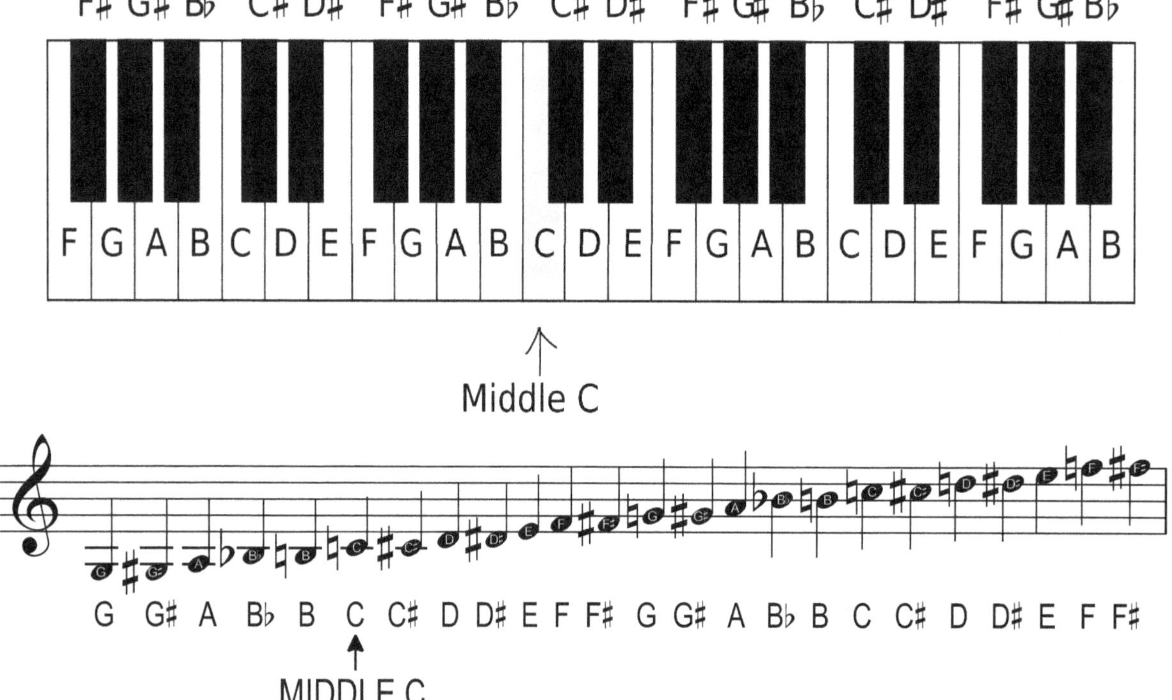

Mary Had a Little Lamb

C
3 2 1 2 3
G
2
C
3 5
Ma - ry had a li - ttle lamb, li - ttle lamb, li - ttle lamb,

3 2 1 2 3 1
G
2
C
3 2 1
Ma - ry had a li - ttle lamb it's fleece was white as snow.

Hot Cross Buns

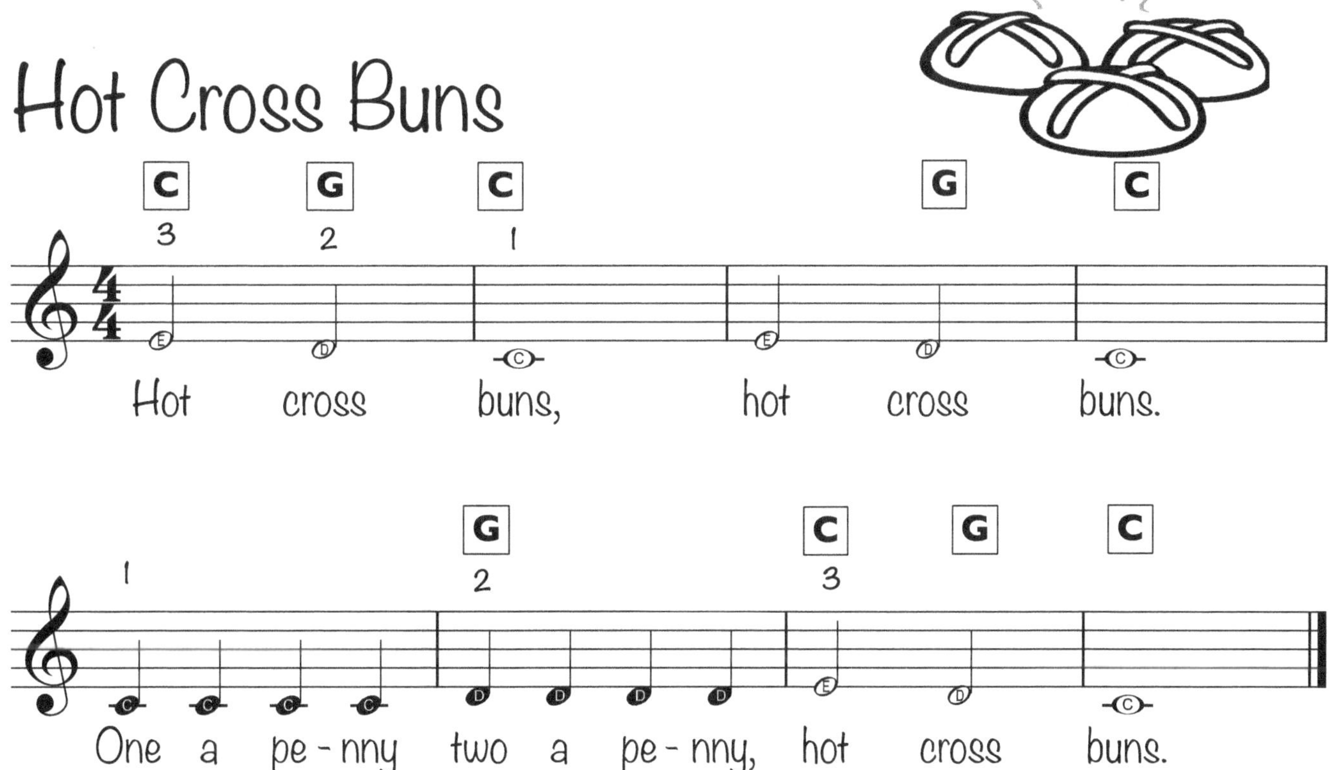

C G C G C
3 2 1
Hot cross buns, hot cross buns.
G C G C
1 2 3
One a pe - nny two a pe - nny, hot cross buns.

Little Bird

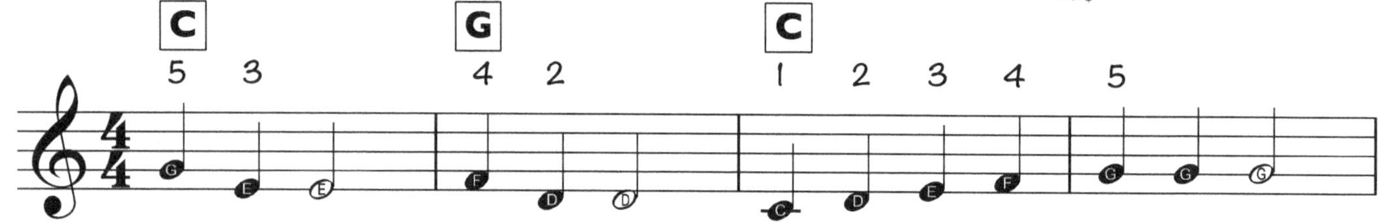

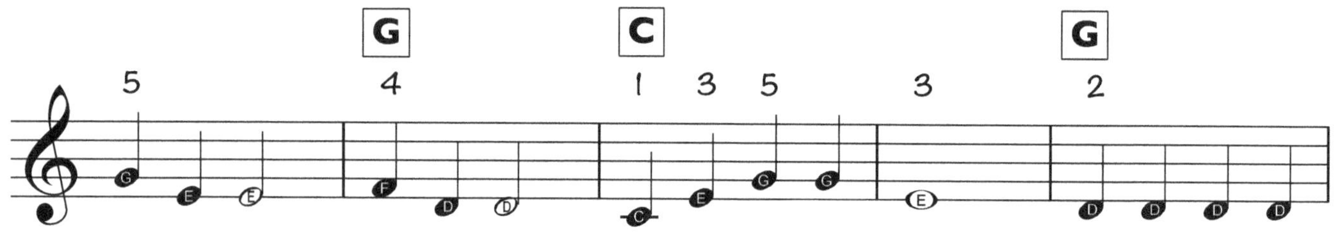

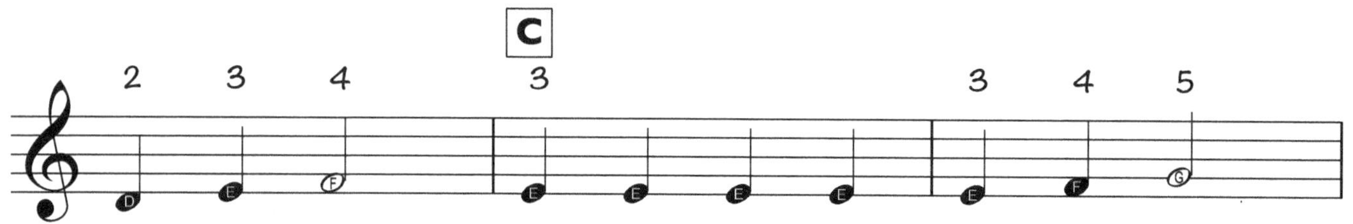

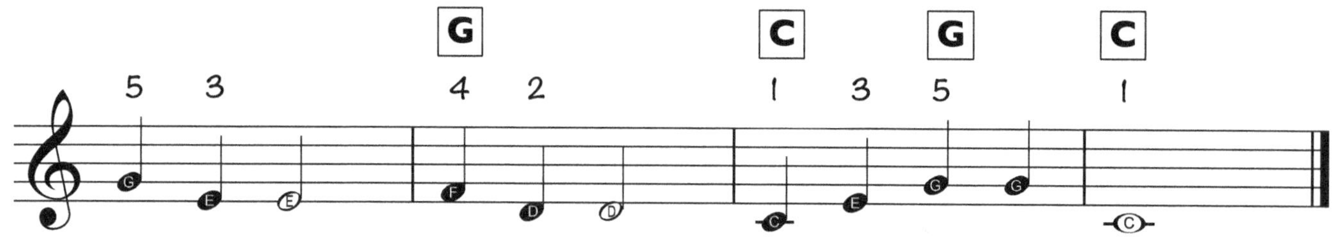

Go and Tell Aunt Dinah

Clown Dance

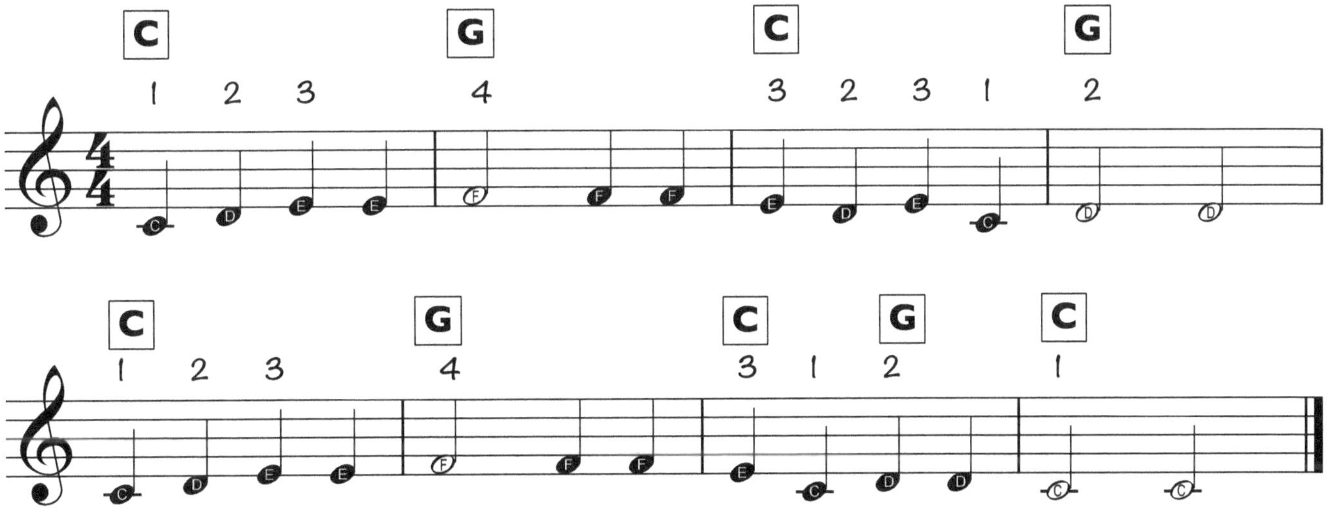

Aura Lee

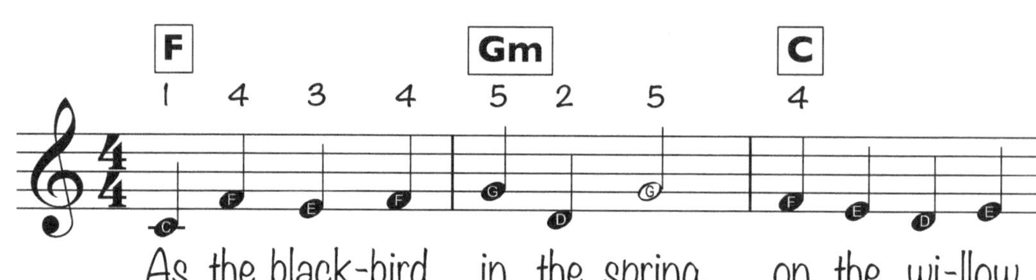

As the black-bird in the spring, on the wi-llow
tree, sat and rocked I heard him sing, sing of Au-ra Lee.

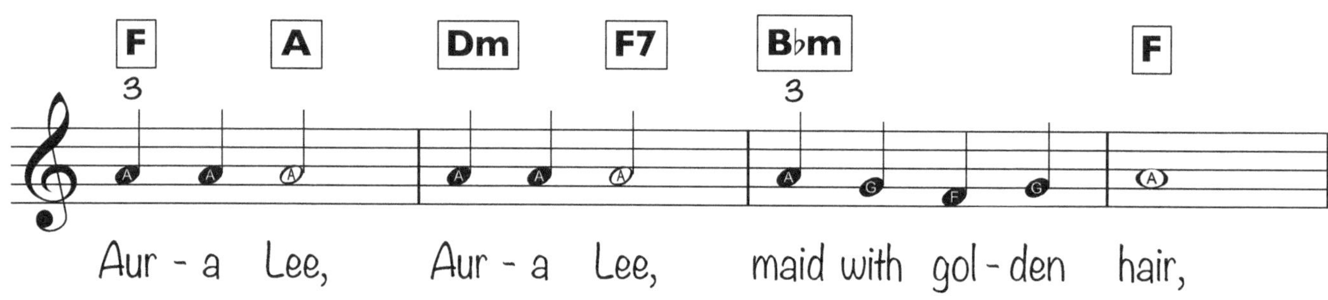

Aur - a Lee, Aur - a Lee, maid with gol-den hair,

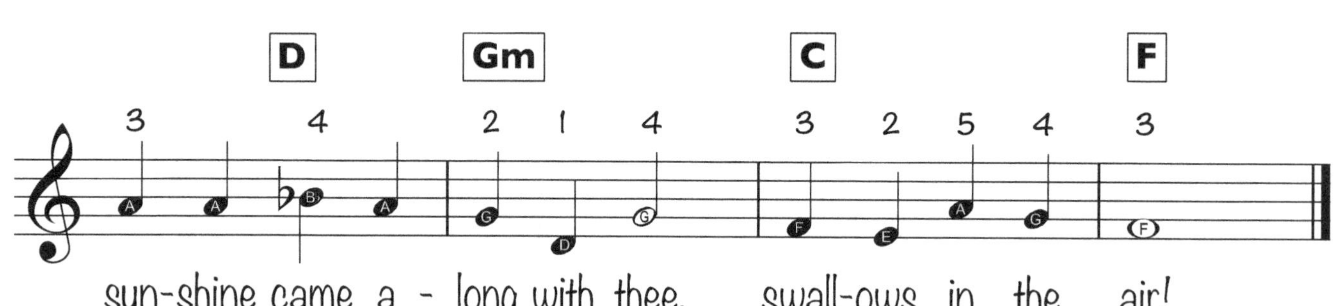

sun-shine came a - long with thee, swall-ows in the air!

Ten Little Indians

One li-ttle two li-ttle three li-ttle In-dians, four li-ttle five li-ttle
six li-ttle In - dians, seven li - ttle eight li - ttle
nine li-ttle In-dians ten li-ttle In-dian boys.

Kum Ba Yah

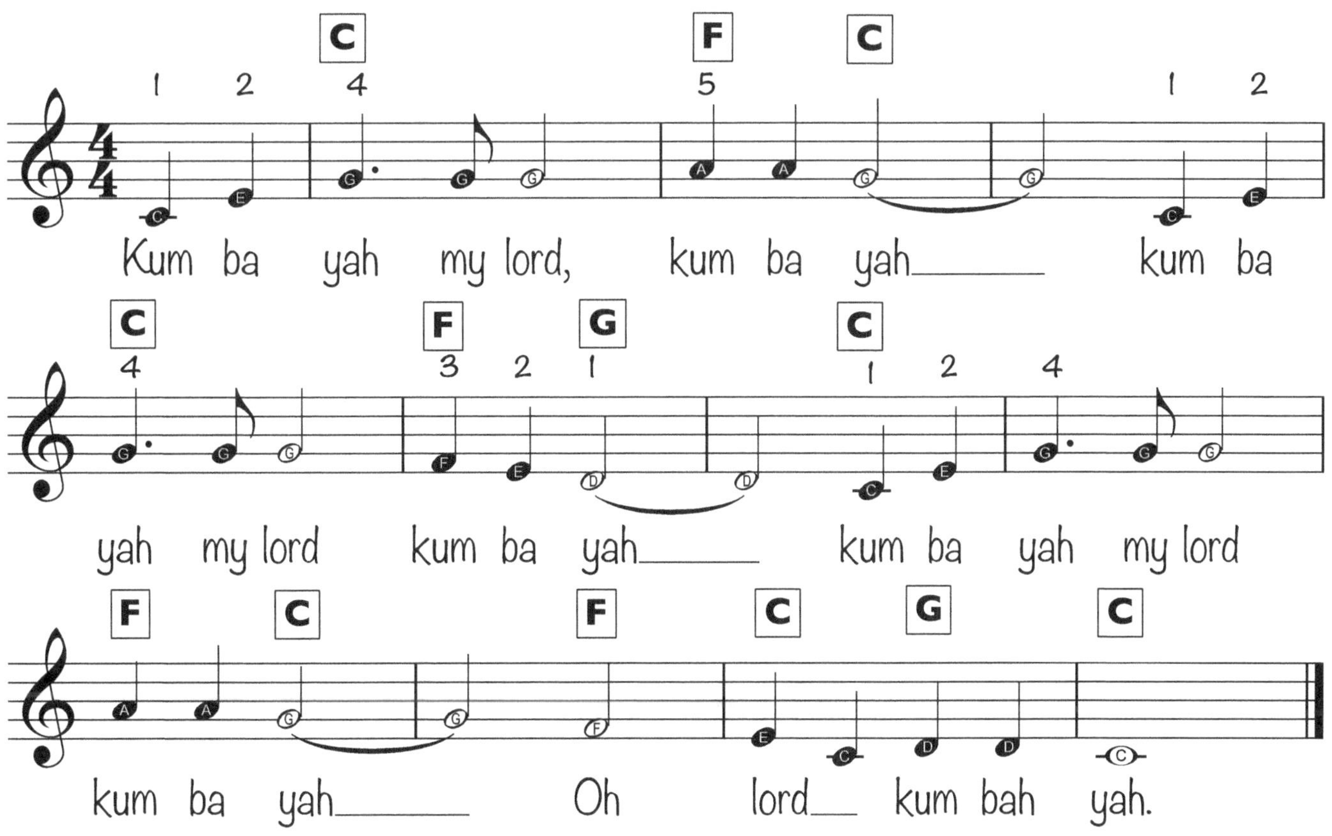

Kum ba yah my lord, kum ba yah_____ kum ba
yah my lord kum ba yah_____ kum ba yah my lord
kum ba yah_____ Oh lord_ kum bah yah.

Old MacDonald had a Farm

F 4   B♭ 1   2   C   F 5   C 4   F 3   1
Old Mac-Don-ald   had a farm,   E I E I O.   And
F 4   B♭ 1   2   C 1   F 5   C   F 1
on that farm he   had some ducks,   E I E I O.   With a
F 4
quack quack here   quack quack there,   here a quack, there a quack,
F
eve - ry - where a quack quack.   Old   Mac - Don - ald
B♭ 2   C   F 5   C 4   F 3
had a farm.   E I E I O.

Ode to Joy

Enroulez le Fils

William Tell

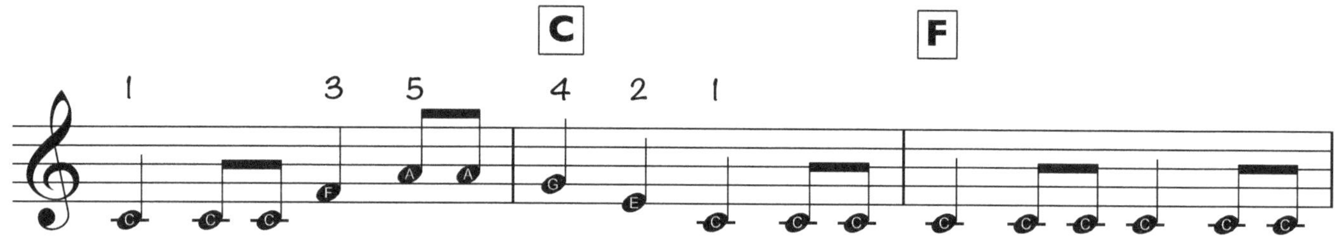

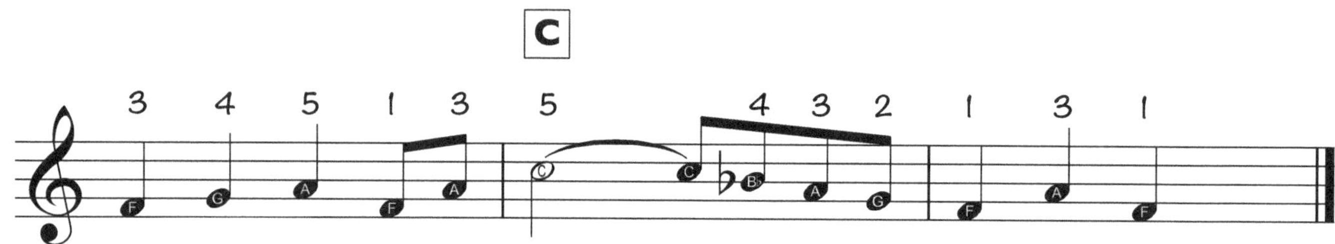

Bluebird

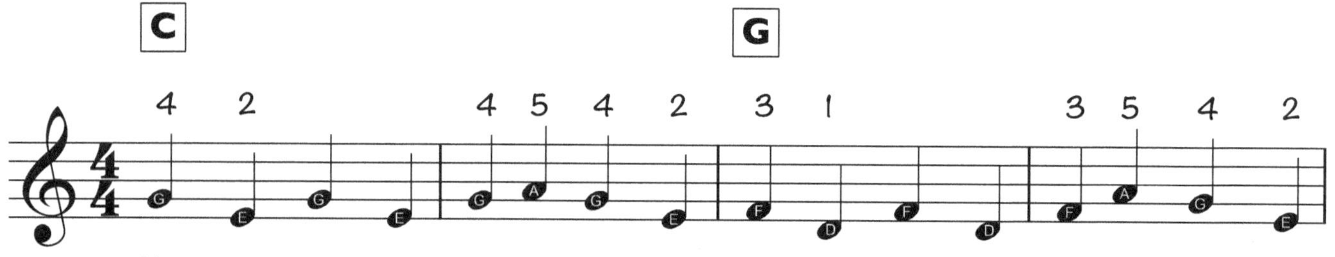
Blue - bird, blue - bird, on my win - dow, blu - bird, blue - bird, on my shoul - der,

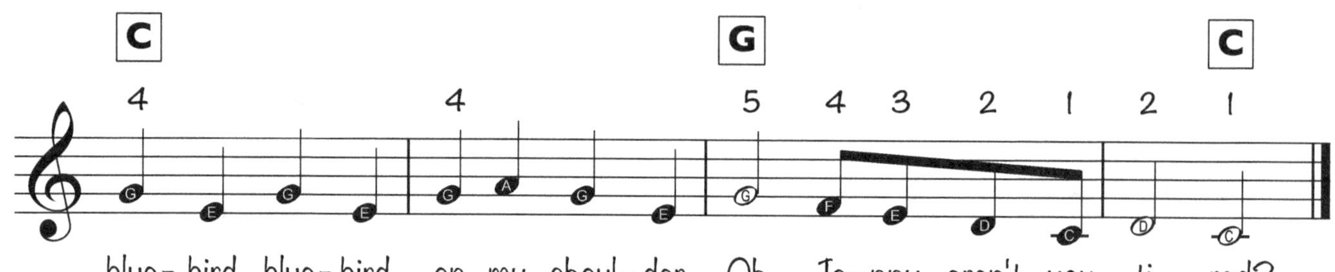
blue - bird, blue - bird on my shoul - der Oh Jo - nny aren't you ti - red?

When the Saints Go Marching In

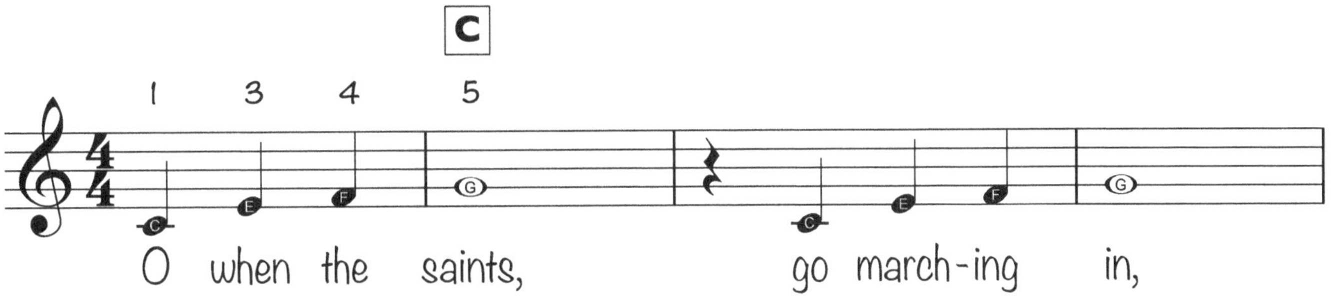
C
1   3   4   5
O when the saints, go march-ing in,

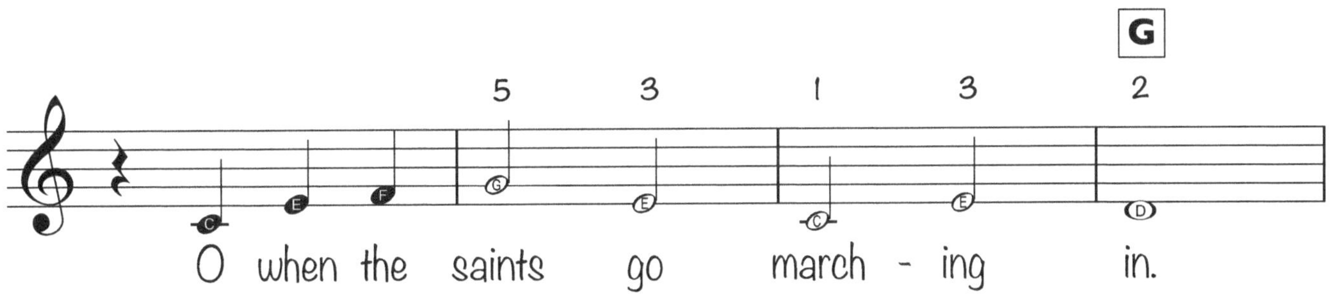
G
5   3   1   3   2
O when the saints go march - ing in.

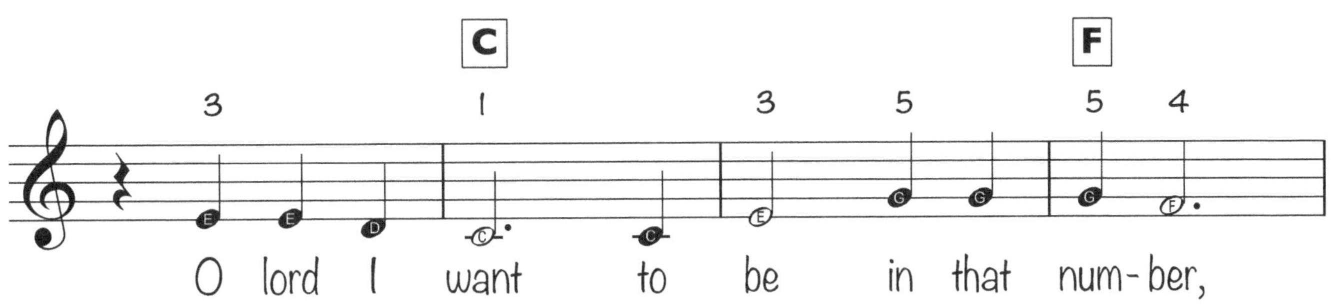
C   F
3   1   3   5   5   4
O lord I want to be in that num-ber,

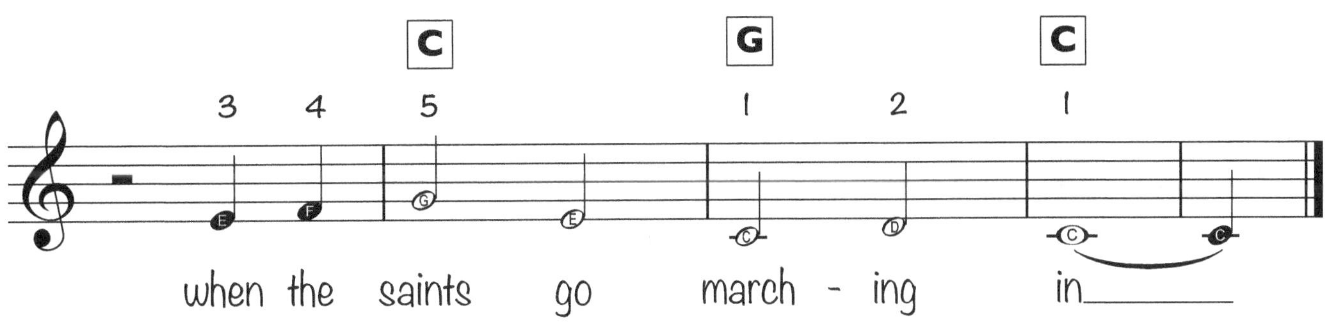
C   G   C
3   4   5   1   2   1
when the saints go march - ing in_____

Twinkle Twinkle Little Star

C 1   4   F 5   C 4   G 4   C 3
Twin - kle, twin - kle, li - ttle star, how I won - der

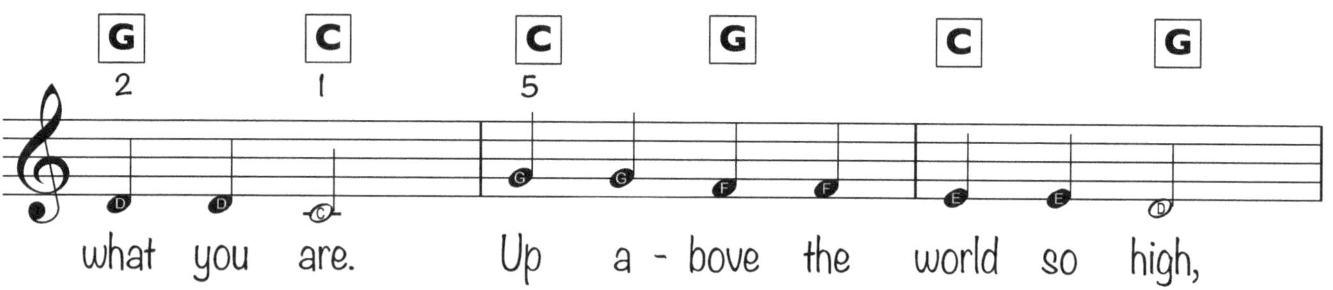

G 2   C 1   C 5   G   C   G
what you are. Up a - bove the world so high,

C   G   C   G   C 1   4
Like a dia - mond in the sky, Twin - kle, twin - kle

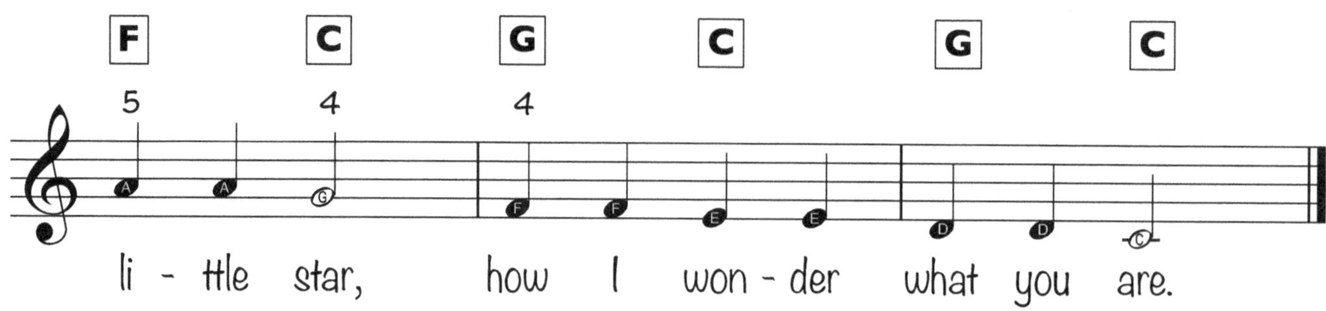

F 5   C 4   G 4   C   G   C
li - ttle star, how I won - der what you are.

Au Clair de la Lune

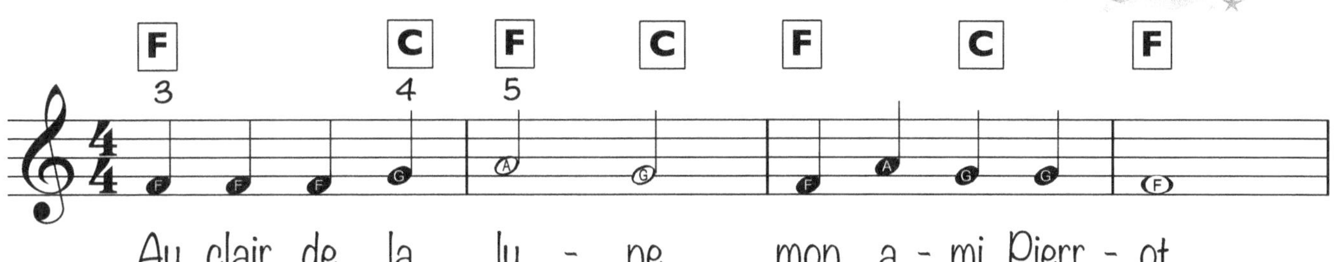

F C F C F C F
3 4 5
Au clair de la lu - ne, mon a - mi Pierr - ot.

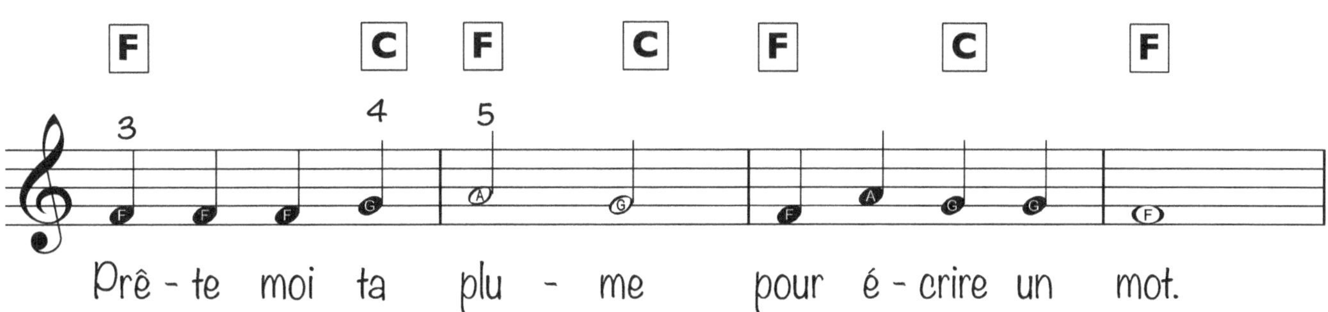

F C F C F C F
3 4 5
Prê - te moi ta plu - me pour é - crire un mot.

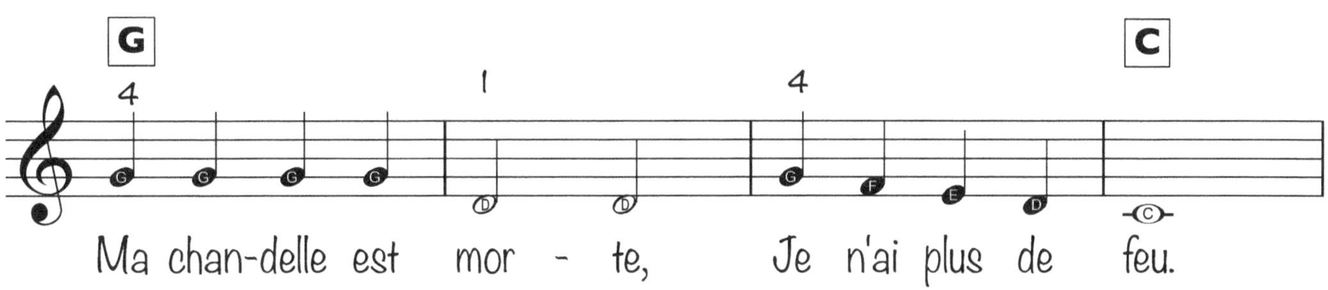

G C
4 1 4
Ma chan-delle est mor - te, Je n'ai plus de feu.

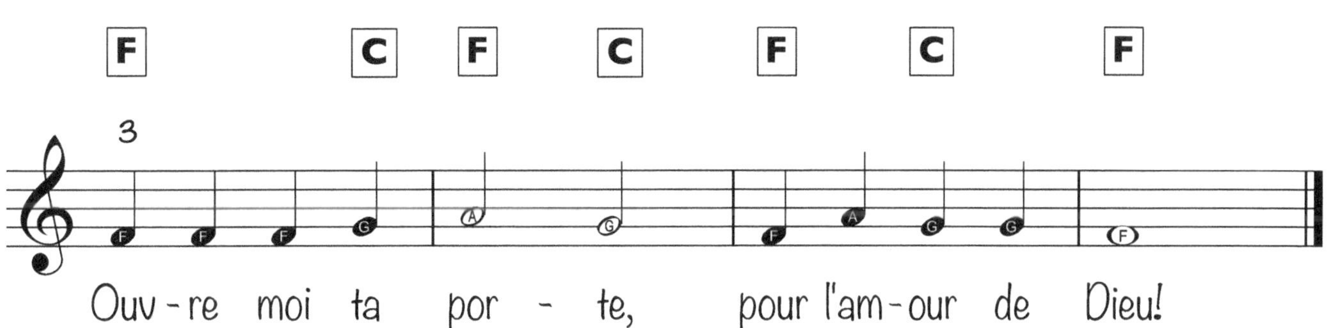

F C F C F C F
3
Ouv -re moi ta por - te, pour l'am-our de Dieu!

¹⁴ Jingle Bells

C
3
Jin - gle bells, jin - gle bells, jin - gle all the way,

G   C   D   G
4   2   5
Oh what fun it is to ride in a once horse o - pen sleigh___

C
3
Jin - gle bells, jin - gle bells, jin - gle all the way,

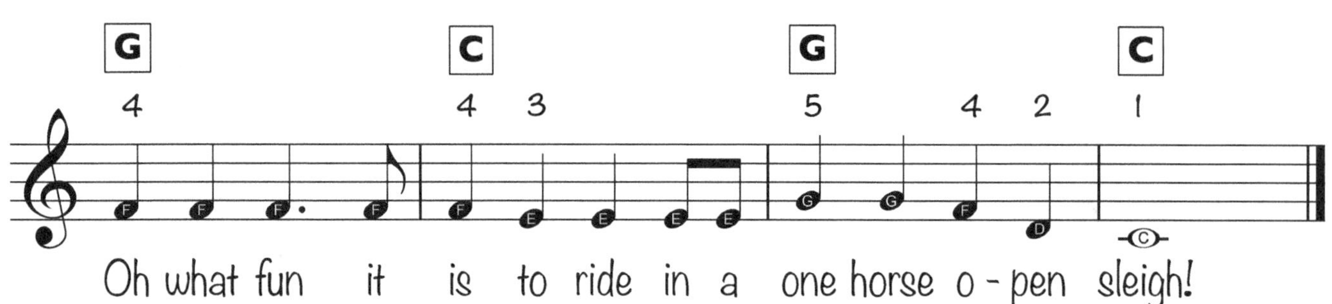

G   C   G   C
4   4 3   5   4 2 1
Oh what fun it is to ride in a one horse o - pen sleigh!

London Bridge is Falling Down

C
4 5 4 3 2
G
1
C
2
Lon - don bridge is   fa - lling down,   fa - lling down,   fa - lling down.
C
4
G
4
C
2 1
Lon - don bridge is   fa - lling down,   my   fair   lady.

Skip to My Lou

C
3 1
G
2 1
Choose your part - ner   skip   to   my Lou,   choose your part - ner
2
4
C
1
skip   to   my   Lou,   choose   your   part - ner
G
C
skip   to   my Lou,   skip   to   my Lou my   dar - lin'.

Michael Row the Boat Ashore

Michael Row the Boat Ashore
C
Mi-chael row the boat a - shore, ha - lle -
F   C   Dm
lu - jah, Mi - chael row the boat a -
G   C   G   C
shore ha - lle - lu_____ jah!
Frère Jacques
C
Frè - re Jac - ques, Frè - re Jac - ques, dor - mez vous,
G   C
dor - mez vous? Sonn - ez les mat - in - es,
G   C   G   C   G   C
sohn-ez les mat-in - es, ding dang dong, ding dang dong!

What Shall we do with the Drunken Sailor?

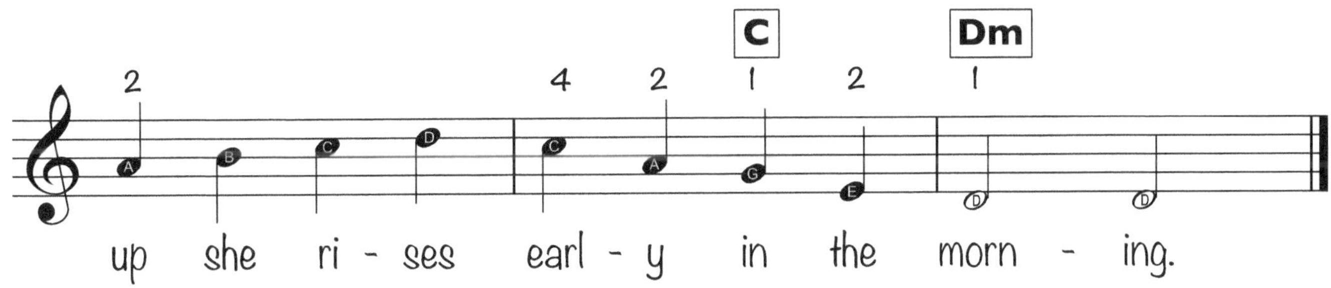

What shall we do with the drunk en sail - or, what shall we do with the
drunk-en sail - or, what shall we do with the drunk-en sail - or
earl - y in the morn - ing? Hoo - ray
up she ris - es, hoo - ray up she ri - ses, hoo - ray
up she ri - ses earl - y in the morn - ing.

Happy Birthday to You

F   C   C   F
Ha-ppy Birth-day to   you,   ha-ppy birth-day to   you,   ha-ppy

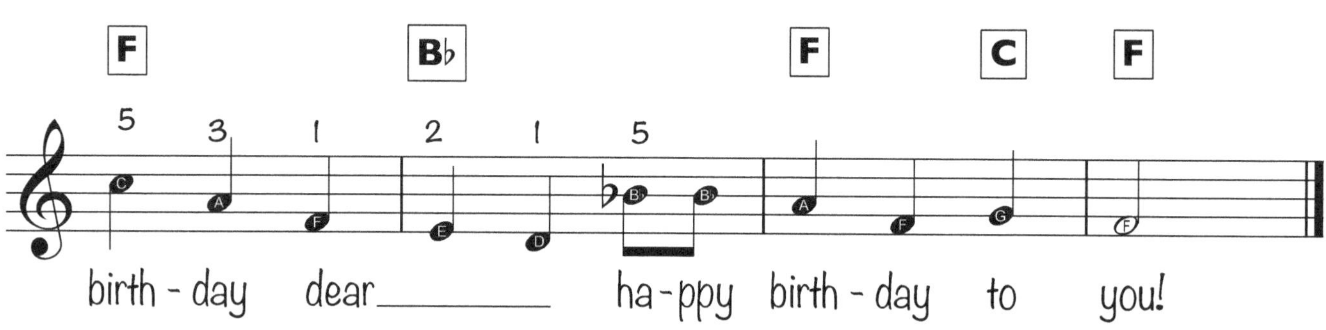

F   Bb   F   C   F
birth - day   dear________   ha-ppy birth - day   to   you!

For He's a Jolly Good Fellow

C   F   C   G
For   he's   a   jo - lly good fe - llow,   for   he's   a

C   F
jo - lly good fe - llow,   for   he's   a   jo - lly good   fe______

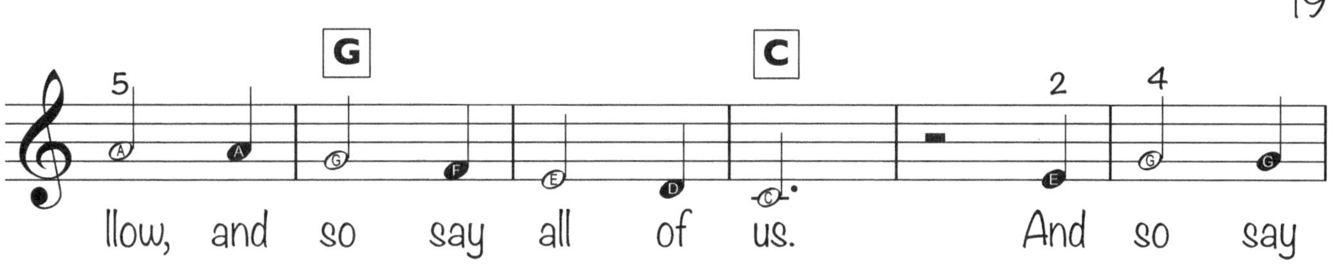

G
C
llow, and so say all of us. And so say

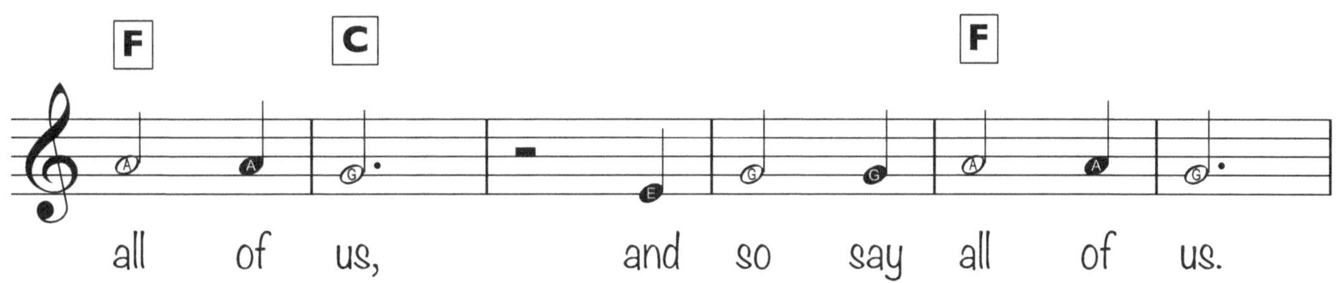

F
C
F
all of us, and so say all of us.

C
F
C
G
O, for he's a jo - lly good fe - llow, for he's a

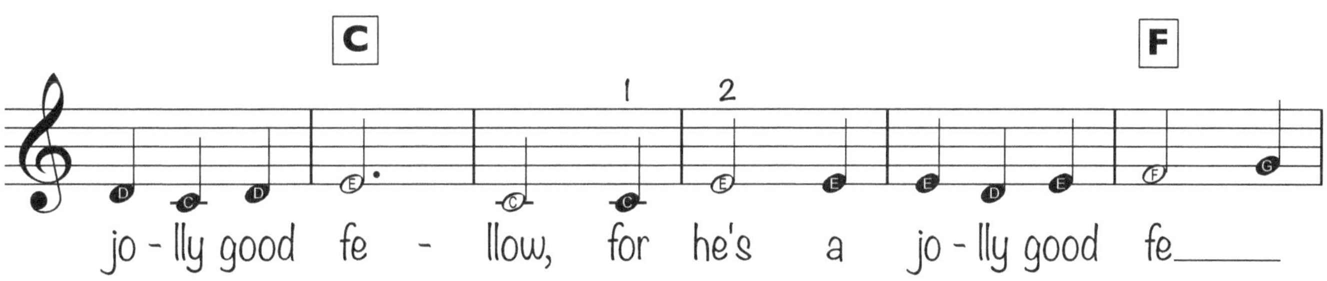

C
F
jo - lly good fe - llow, for he's a jo - lly good fe_____

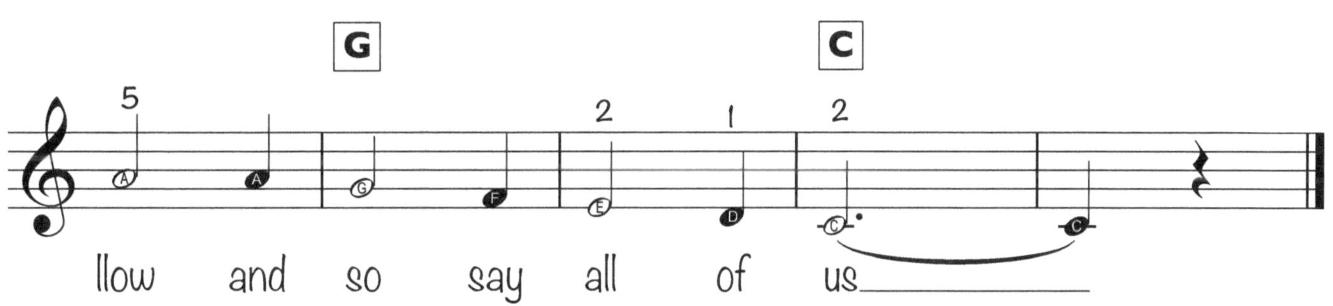

G
C
llow and so say all of us_________

The Can Can

C
G7
C
1
2   4
5
4   5   2
C
D   F   E   D
G   G
G   A   E   F

G7
C
G7
1
1   4
1   5
1   3   2
D   D
D   F   E   D
C   B   A
G   F   E   D
C

C
G7
C
1
4
4   5
C
D   F   E   D
G   G
G   A   E   F
G7
C
G7
C
1   4   3   2
D   D
D   F   E   D
C   D   E   C
G

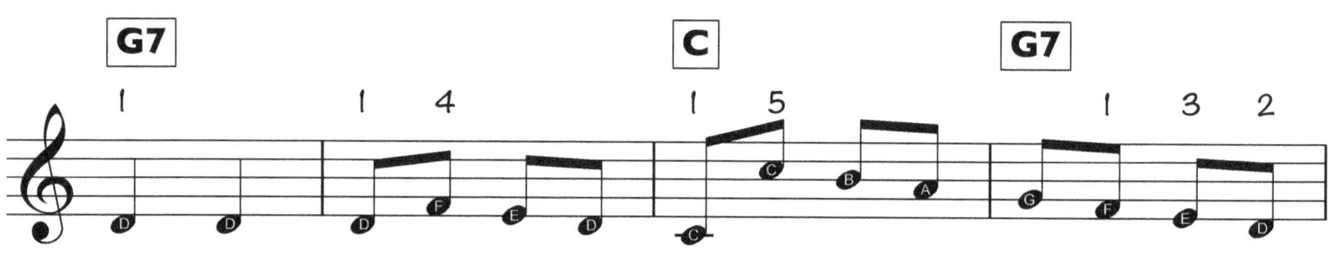

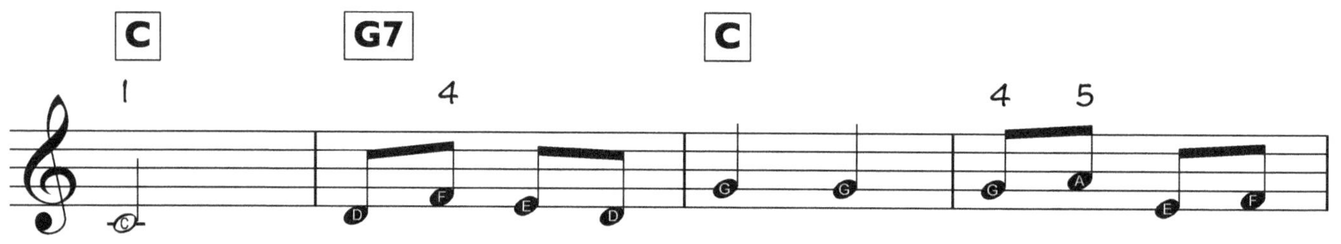

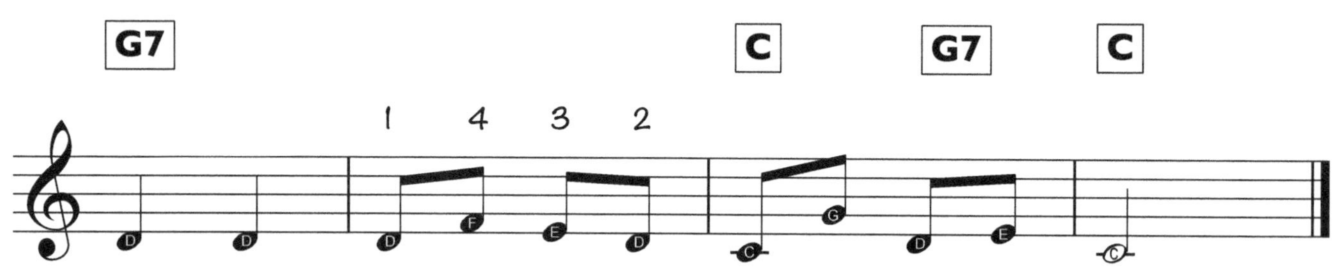

This Old Man

C   F
This Old Man, he played one, he played knick knack

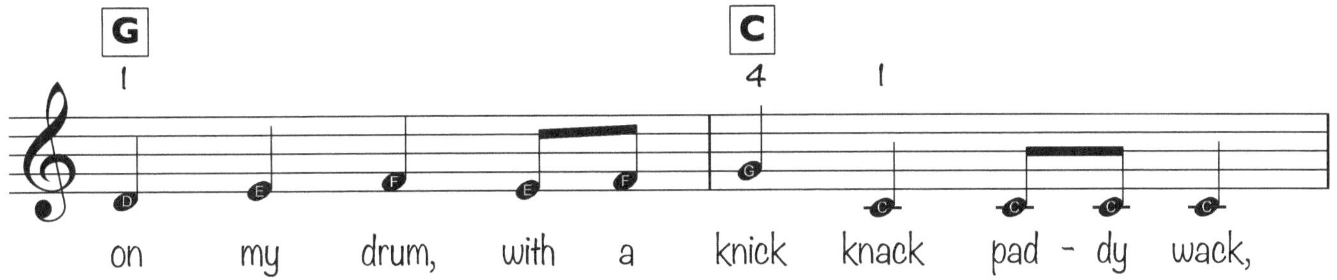

G   C
on my drum, with a knick knack pad - dy wack,

G   C G C
give a dog a bone, this old man came roll - ing home!

The Muffin Man

F   Gm   C
Have you seen the Muff-in Man, the Muff-in Man, the Muff-in Man,

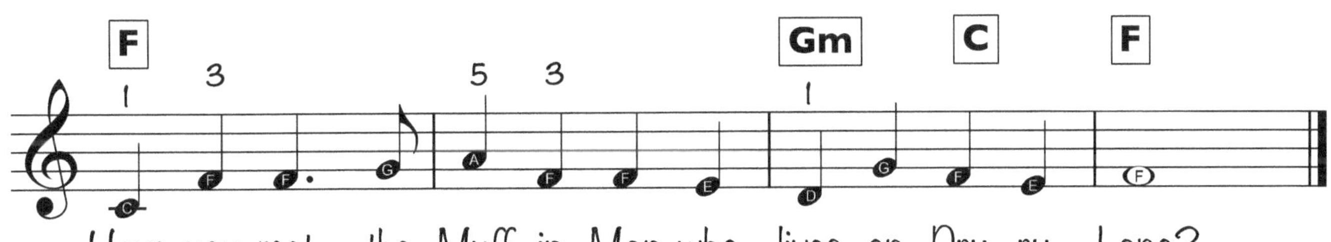

F   Gm   C   F
Have you met the Muff-in Man who lives on Dru-ry Lane?

A Tisket, a Tasket

C
A tis - ket, a tas - ket, a green and yel-low bas - ket, I

G7
C
sent a let - ter to my friend and on the way I dropped it; I

dropped it, I dropped it, yes on the way I dropped it; a

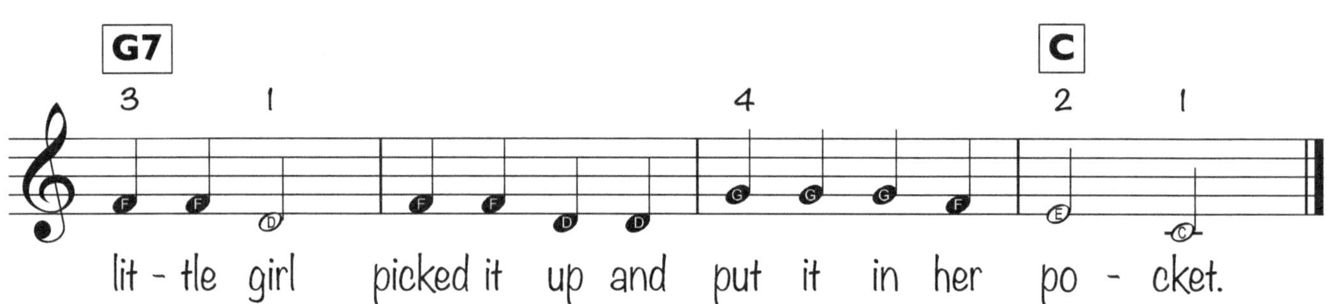

G7
C
lit - tle girl picked it up and put it in her po - cket.

Lavender's Blue

Lav - en - der's blue di - lly di - lly, lav - en - der's green.

When you are King di - lly di - lly I will be Queen.

Scarborough Fair

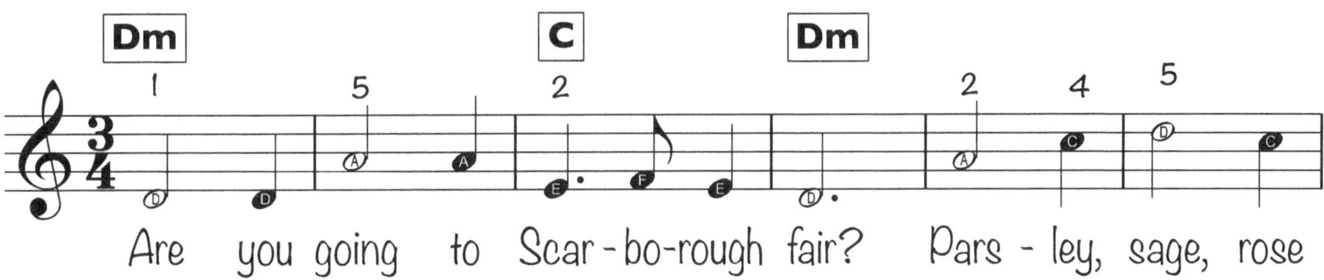

Are you going to Scar - bo - rough fair? Pars - ley, sage, rose

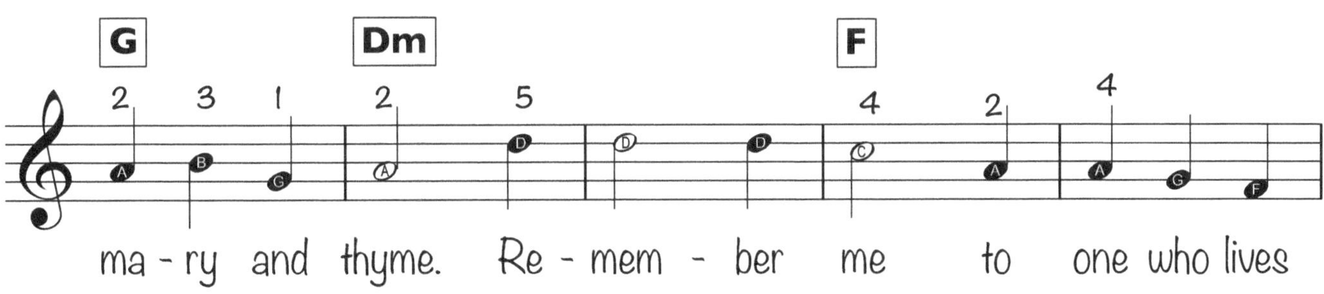

ma - ry and thyme. Re - mem - ber me to one who lives

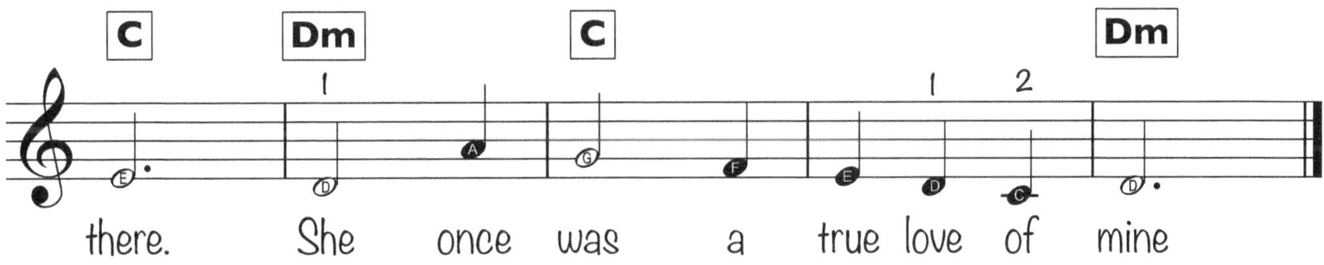

there. She once was a true love of mine

My Bonnie Lies Over the Ocean

My Bonn - ie lies o - ver the
o - cean, my Bonn - ie lies
o - ver the sea, my Bonn - ie lies
o - ver the o - cean, o bring back my
Bonn - ie to me. Bring

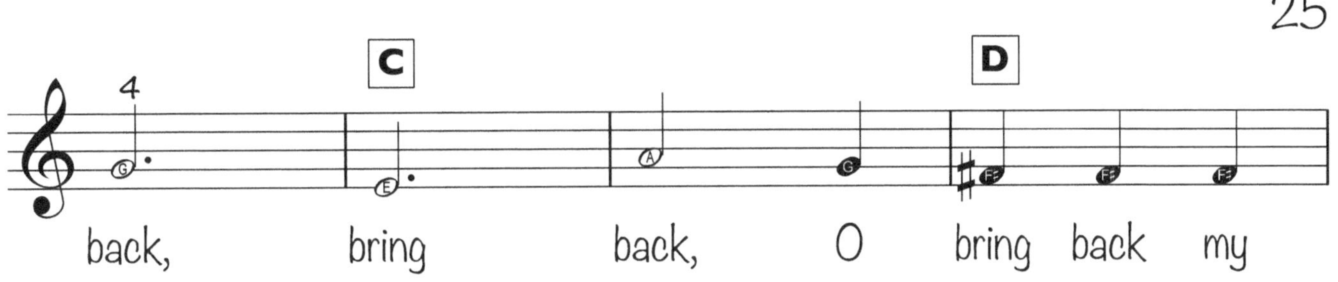
C
D
back, bring back, O bring back my

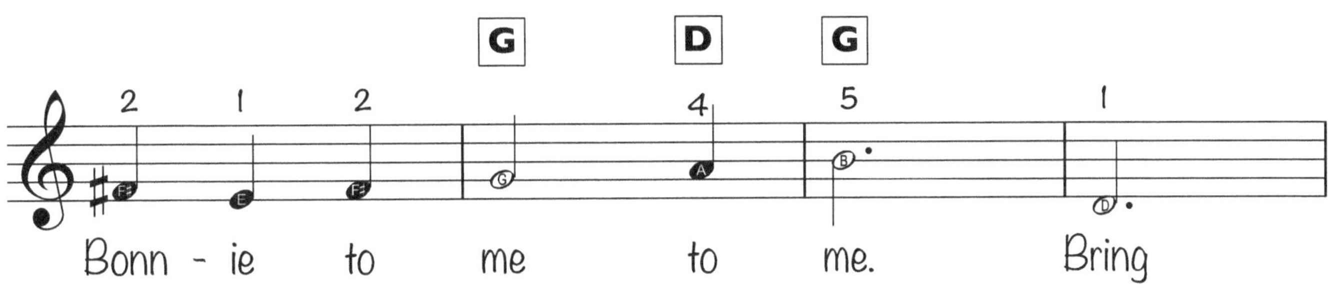
G D G
Bonn - ie to me to me. Bring

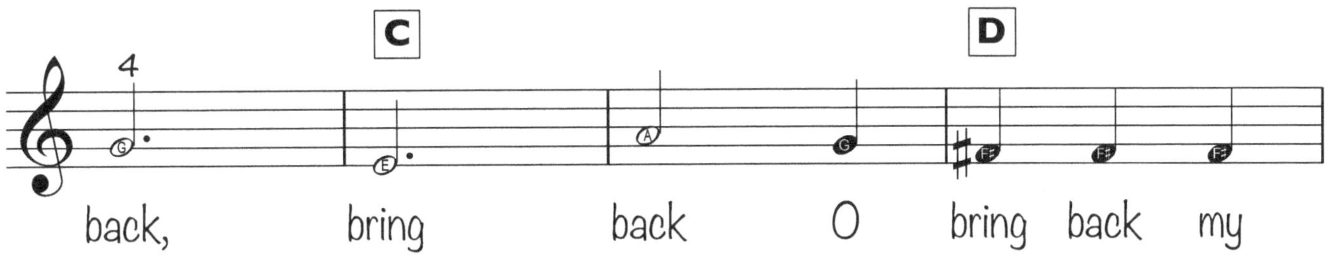
C
D
back, bring back O bring back my

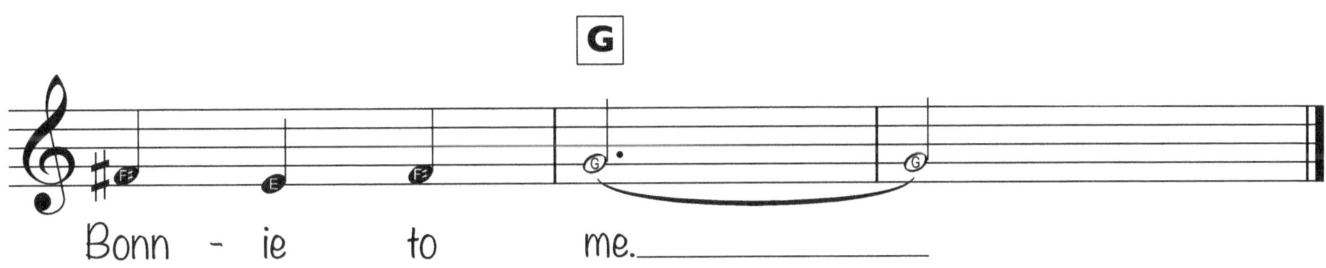
G
Bonn - ie to me.

She'll be Comin' Round the Mountain

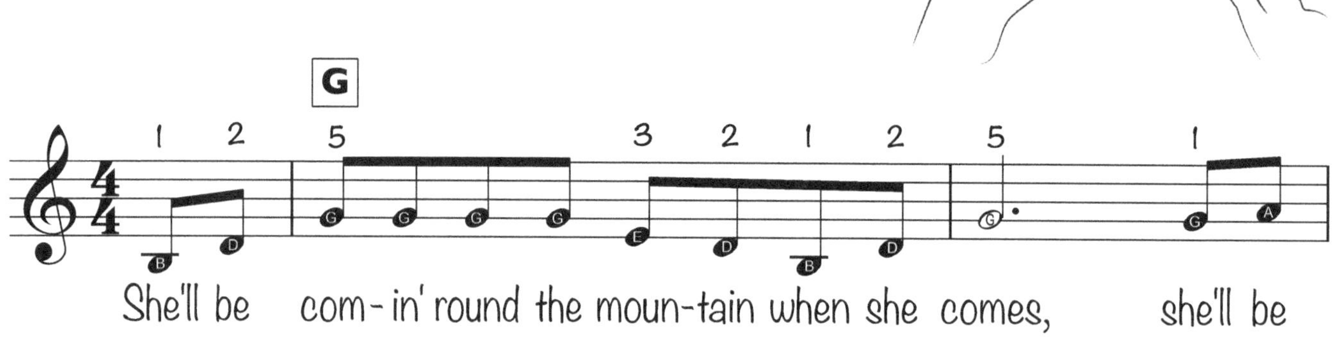

G
She'll be com-in' round the moun-tain when she comes, she'll be

D
com-in' round the moun-tain when she comes. She'll be

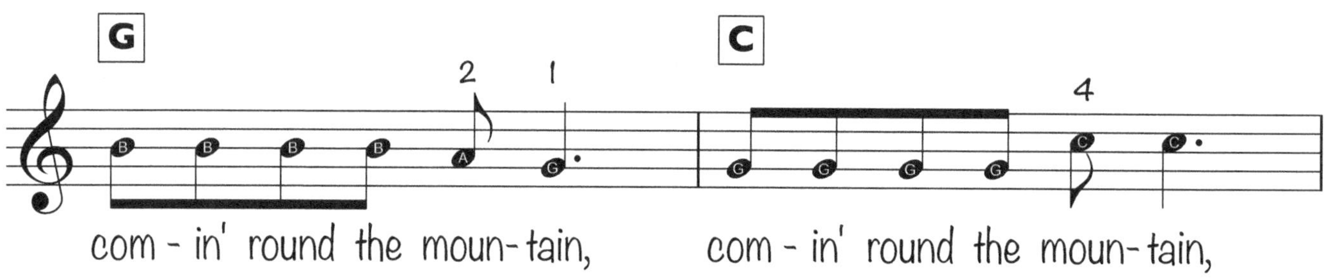

G   C
com-in' round the moun-tain, com-in' round the moun-tain,

G   D   G
com-in' round the moun-tain when she comes.

Good King Wenceslas

27
F C F C
Good King Wen - ces - las looked out,
Bb C F C F C
on the feast of Ste - phen. When the snow lay round a-bout,
Bb C F F C F Dm
deep and crisp and e - ven. Bright-ly shone the moon that night,
Bb C F F Bb
though the frost was cru - el, when a poor man
Dm C F C Dm Bb F
came in sight, gath-ring win - ter fu______ el.

O My Darlin', Clementine

F
3 | 1 | 5 | 3 | 1
Oh my dar - lin', oh my dar - lin', oh my
C   C
5 | 2 | 4
dar - lin' Clem - en - tine, Thou art lost and gone for-
F   Dm   Gm   C   F
3 | 1 | 4 | 3 | 1 | 2 | 4 | 3
ev - er, dread-ful sor - ry Clem - en - tine!

Amazing Grace

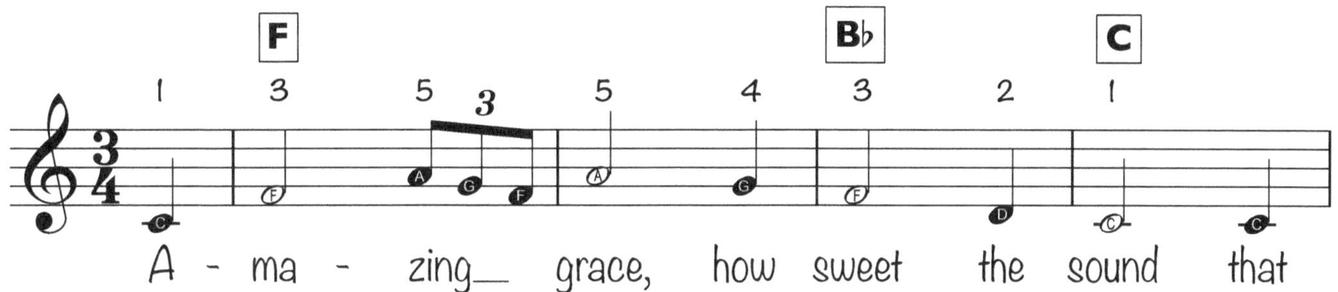

F
B♭
C
A - ma - zing__ grace, how sweet the sound that

F
C
saved a___ wretch like__ me__________ I___

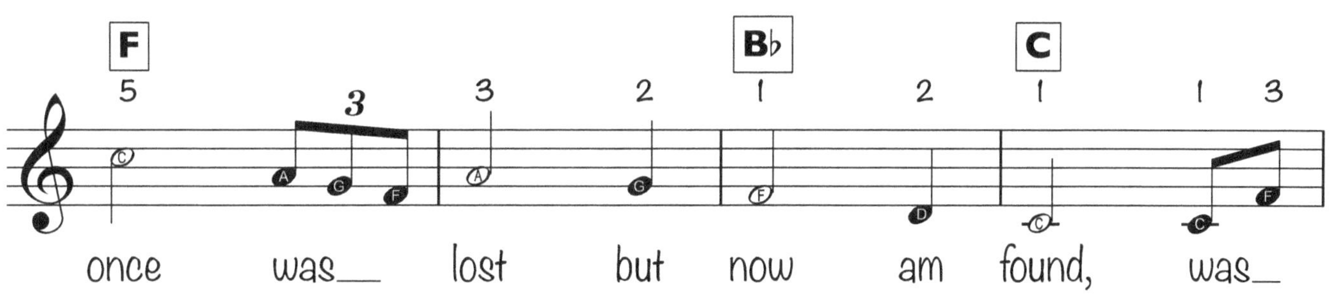

F
B♭
C
once was__ lost but now am found, was__

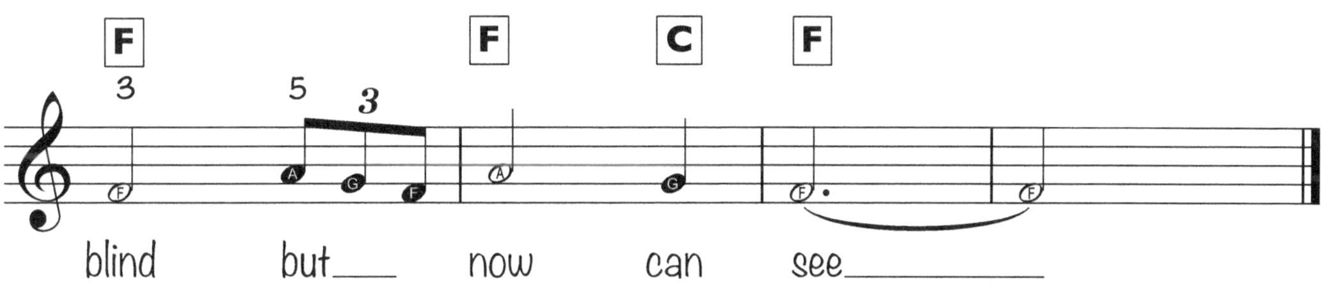

F
F
C
F
blind but___ now can see__________

Greensleeves

Em
D
A - las my love____ you do me
C
wrong____ to cast me off____ dis -
B
Em
court - eous - ly, for I have loved____ you
D
C
well and long____ de - light - ing
B
Em
in____ your com - pan - y.

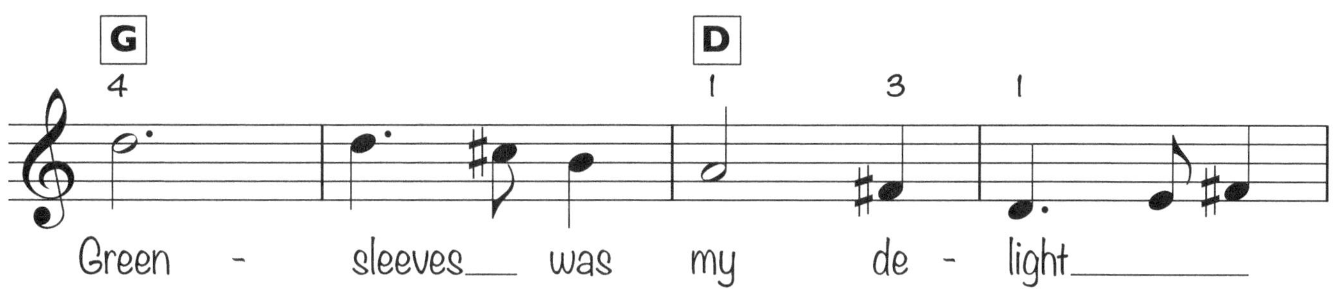
G
D
Green - sleeves___ was my de - light_______

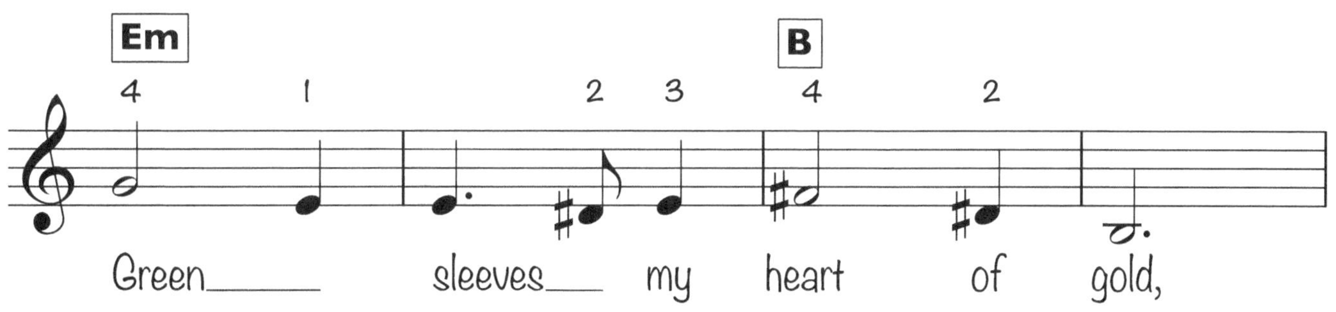
Em
B
Green_____ sleeves___ my heart of gold,

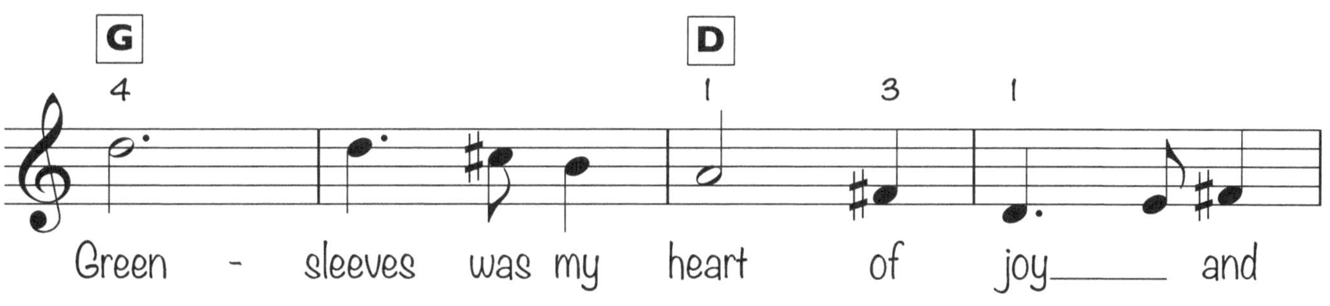
G
D
Green - sleeves was my heart of joy____ and

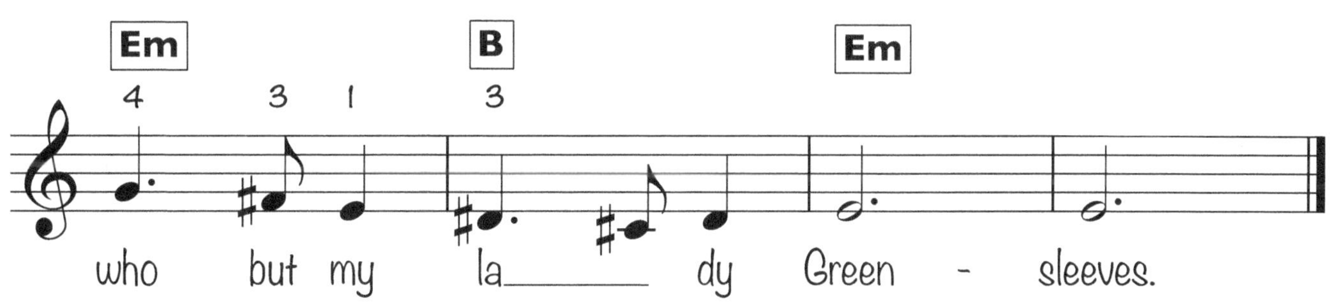
Em
B
Em
who but my la_____ dy Green - sleeves.

Home on the Range

F
Bb
O give me a home where the buff - a - lo roam, where the

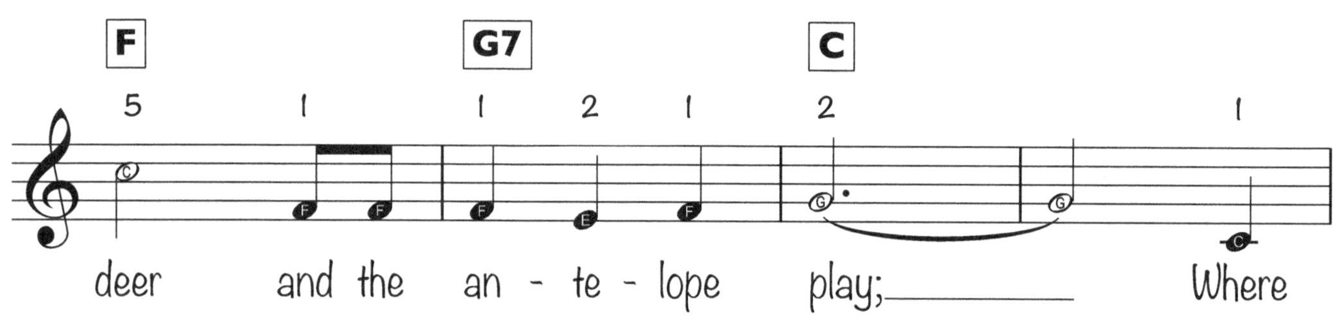
F
G7
C
deer and the an - te - lope play;_______ Where

F
Bb
sel - dom is heard a dis - cour - ag - ing word and the

F
C7
F
skies are not clou - dy all day_______

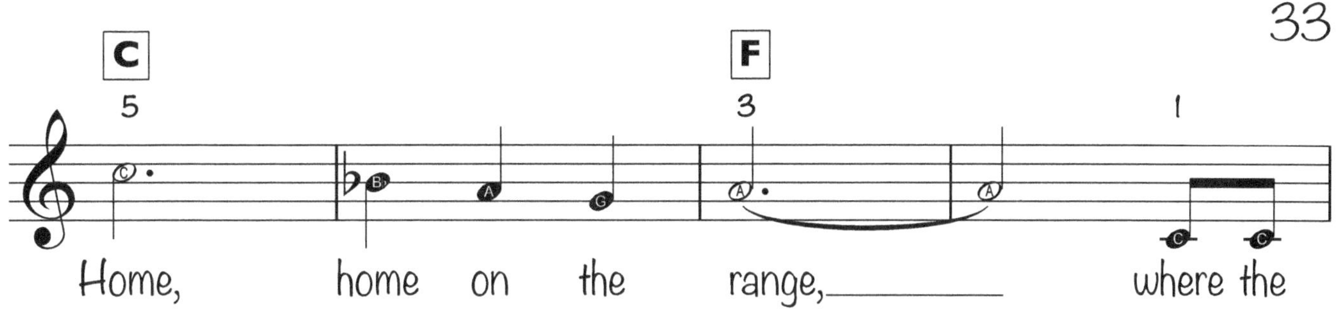
C
F
Home, home on the range,________ where the

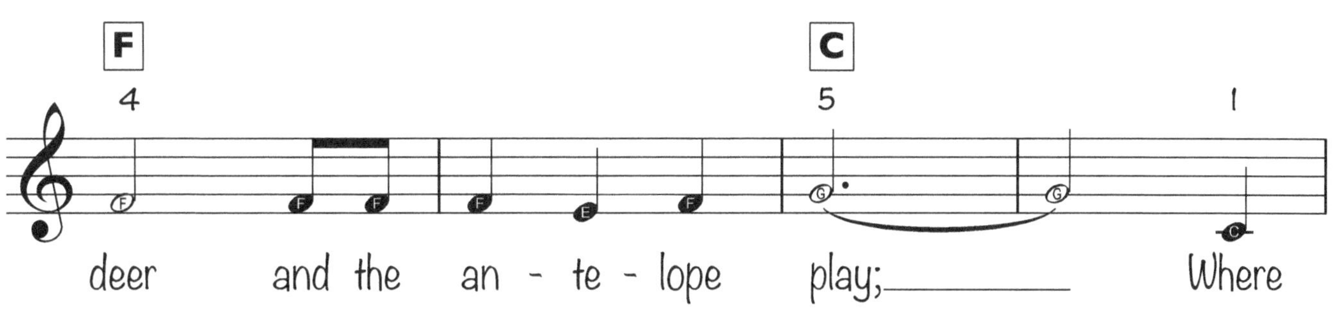
F
C
deer and the an - te - lope play;________ Where

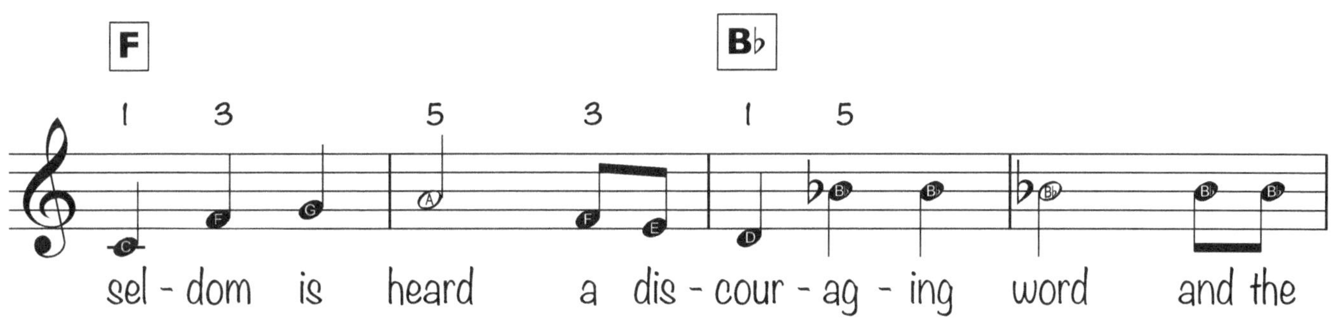
F
B♭
sel - dom is heard a dis - cour - ag - ing word and the

F
C7
F
skies are not clou - dy all day________

Away in a Manger

F C F
A - way in a___ man-ger no___

Gm C7
crib for a bed, the___ li - ttle lord

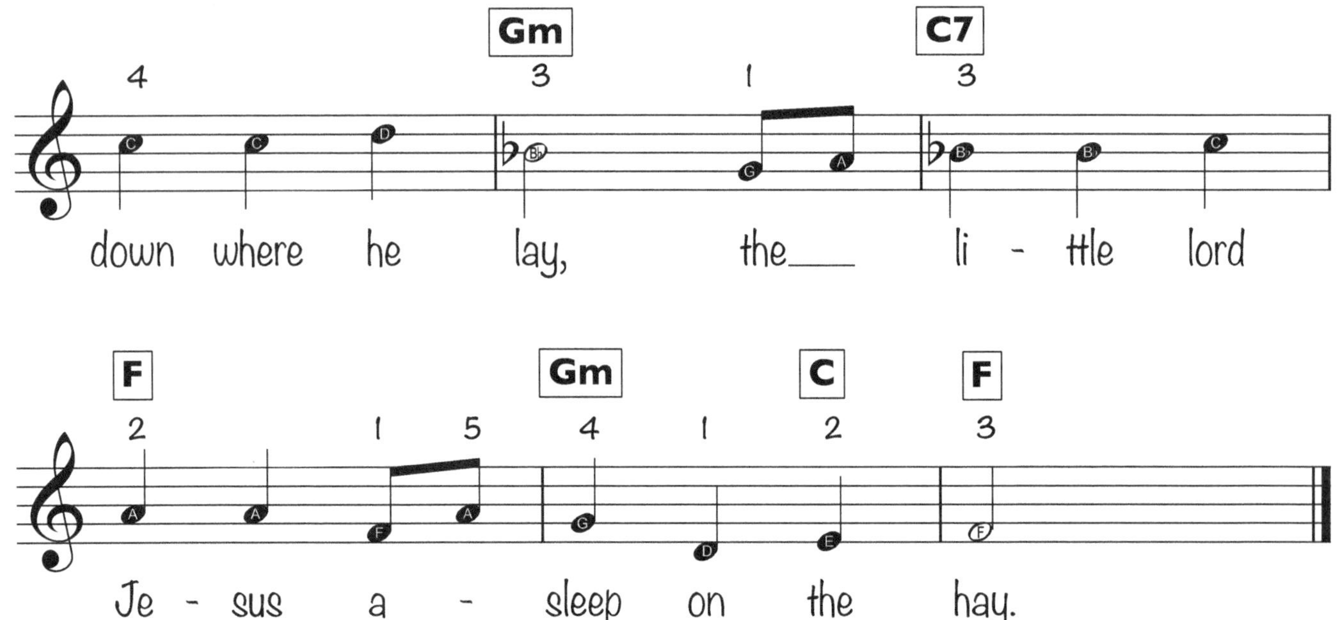

F G C F C F
Je-sus laid___ down his sweet head. The stars in the___ bright sky looked

Gm C7
down where he lay, the____ li - ttle lord

F Gm C F
Je - sus a - sleep on the hay.

Little Brown Jug

C F
My wife and I live all a-lone in a
G C
li-ttle log hut we called our own. She loves gin and
F G C
I love rum and don't we have a lot of fun.
F G C
Ha ha ha, hee hee hee, li-ttle brown jug don't I love thee,
F G C
ha ha ha, hee hee hee, li-ttle brown jug don't I love thee.

The Skye Boat Song

G Em C D
Speed bonn-ie boat like a bird on the wing,
G C D
On - ward the sail - ors cry
G Em C D
Ca - rry the lad that's born to be King
G C D
o - ver the sea to Skye
Em Am
Loud the winds howl, loud the waves roar,
Em B Em
thun - der clouds rend the air

Em
Am
Baff - led our foes stand on the shore,
Em
B
Em
D
foll - ow they will not dare.
G
Em
C
D
Speed bonn-ie boat like a bird on the wing,
G
C
D
On - ward the sail - ors cry
G
Em
C
D
Ca - rry the lad that's born to be King
G
C
G
o - ver the sea to Skye!

Lullaby

C
G
1 3 1 2 5 3 2 1
E E G E E G E G C B A A G D E
Lu-lla by, and good night, go to bed now and sleep tight, close your

C
1 2 5 3 4 5 1
F D D E F D F B A G B C C C
eyes__ start to yawn, pleas-ant dreams un-til the dawn. Close your

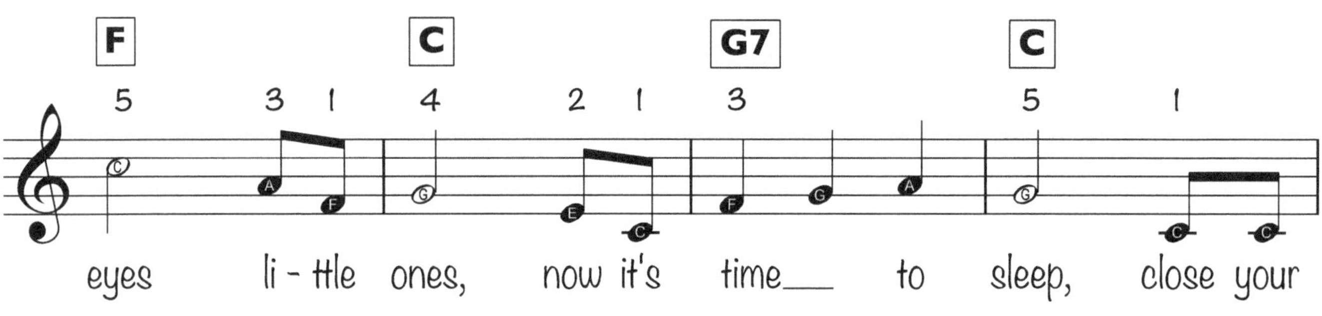
F C G7 C
5 3 1 4 2 1 3 5 1
C A F G E C F G A G C C
eyes li-ttle ones, now it's time__ to sleep, close your

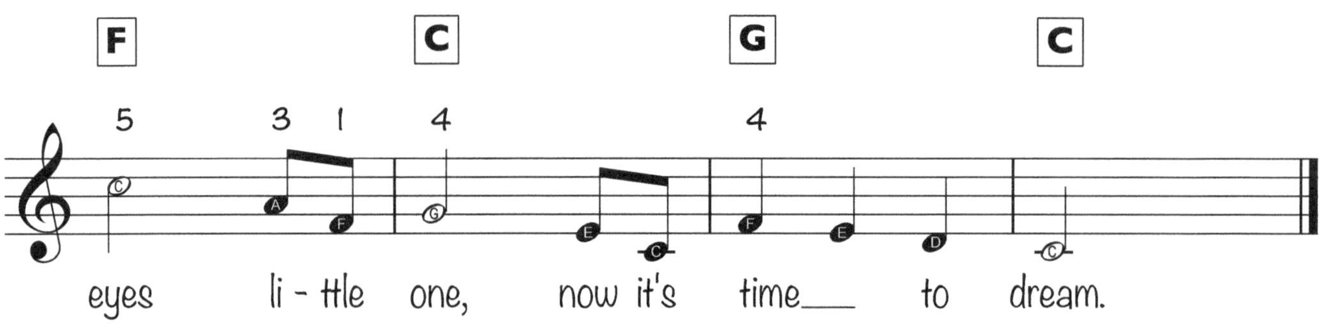
F C G C
5 3 1 4 4
C A F G E C F E D C
eyes li-ttle one, now it's time__ to dream.

Chord shapes

Above the melody line of each of the tunes you will see letters which tell you what chord you should play with each section of the melody. The chart below shows you how to play each of the chords used in this book.

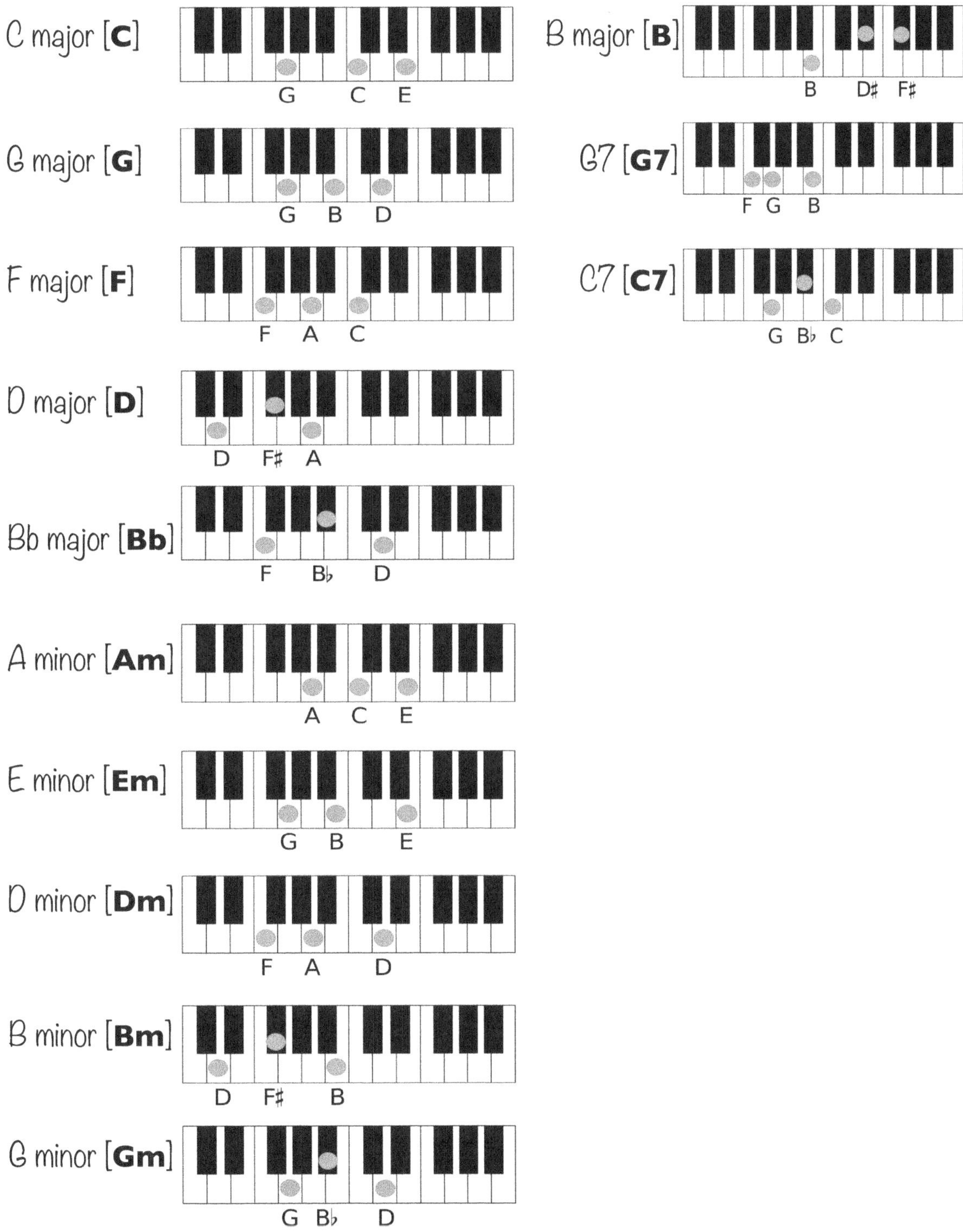

More books for young musicians

Young musicians will love these exciting books that have been designed to make practice fun and easy!

CHRISTMAS SONGS for PIANO

CHRISTMAS
Songs for Piano

Get into the mood for Christmas with these great melodies!
A selection of 24 popular Christmas carols arranged for piano. The first few songs are really easy and the difficulty level gradually increases through the book. These beautiful tunes are suitable for children, beginners or adults.

PICCOLO PIANO

A lovely selection of easy tunes presented in clear print and with colourful illustrations:

40 TUNES
Piccolo Piano
Easy Piano & Keyboard Songs for Kids
including tips on how to play

- simple, well known melodies
- letter names for each note
- hints for which fingers to use
- tunes playable with right hand only
- note reference chart and instruction on how to find the notes and read the music
- tunes arranged in order of difficulty

MUSIC MANUSCRIPT BOOK

Music Manuscript Book
36 pages - 6 large staves per page

Kids love learning to draw treble and bass clefs and can take their first steps in music composition with this fun little manuscript book. Six large staves on each page make this super easy for littlies to use.